GW00459288

Gallery Books
Editor: Peter Fallon

THE SKY DIDN'T FALL

Kerry Hardie

THE SKY DIDN'T FALL

Gallery Books

The Sky Didn't Fall
is first published
simultaneously in paperback
and in a clothbound edition
on 26 June 2003.

The Gallery Press
Loughcrew
Oldcastle
County Meath
Ireland

ISBN 1 85235 348 1 (*paperback*)
1 85235 349 X (*clothbound*)

A CIP catalogue record for this book
is available from the British Library.

The Gallery Press acknowledges the financial assistance
of An Chomhairle Ealaíon / The Arts Council, Ireland.

Contents

in memory of my father
Paddy Jolley

Rivers

for Pat

After the frost-locked week
the grey day eases open like a hand;
the river gleams, the sally stems flare red.

You tell me how you reached that place at night
and, in the morning, in your bed,
opened the guide book, read
of the town's siting at the narrowest place.
Outside, the Orinoco and its mile-wide stretch.

Sweat flutes the printed page.
A metal bedstead, thrown-down bags.
Your face there, face here.

A heron standing in the long shine of the weir.

View from Inside the House

The light behind the corner of that building.
The rowan.
The pattern of bricks in the wall.

In that house
your life quivered.

It's there yet,
though not the body you wore.

There, at the foot of the stairs,
where you paused on your way to the door:

that moment of not knowing if you're able
for the darkness of a form against the light.

The rectangle, framing the world.
The light behind the figure,

streaming in.

All Lives Know Longing, All Lives are Contained

for Ann O'Regan

It is early in March.
A dish on the sill bears a cracked glaze
and a cargo of hyacinth bulbs.
The chestnut outside the window
holds swollen buds to the sky,
the mistle thrush in its branches
grooms feathers, slick and strong.

You watch, lick at your finger,
smooth the boned arcs of your brows.
The light strengthens
and sits on the dish and the tree.
The unplanted bulbs
are greening themselves from within.
You've let their time pass this year,
their time and the thrust of their scent
in January's closed rooms.
You look where that hill falls away
and the other one stands blue behind it.
That's where the sun sets today;
in August it slides down the sky further west
and drops to the back of the ridge
like the letter you slid down the crack in the boards
and carefully never retrieved.
You have always looked out through this window,
past the slope of the roof and the oak.
Sweet and strong.
With your right index finger
you stir the green shoots in the dish.

That Call Again

Spring walks North,
two miles every hour —

To follow her bare footprints in the mud,
eyes starred with pierce of stars on blackthorn,

with stab of stars
on fresh black stretch of night.

Such anarchy of amble stops the heart.
To loose the busy seeds pooled in the palm,

to leave down the fork, let the rake lie —
And not one dazed glance back,

nor thought for the warm darkness
that waits behind the door left standing open.

The Day of the Funeral

for Sheena

She sent me on errands because I was annoying the kitchen.
My sister and my sister-in-law doing food.
Roasting tins and meat and knives.

When I got back you were there, just off the plane.
You had missed out on seeing him with the rest of us,
so together we drove to the church.

Quiet there. December light.
The long box stretched before the altar.
Your arm about me and mine about you.

And we laughed because it was only the three of us,
like sitting at the kitchen table, talking.
We knew, of course, but we had him all around us.

That was one of the best things about that day.
You and I, playing Mary,
while the others did Martha.

After a While, We Go In

I wait,
use the stick that he made,
wear the scarf that he wore,
watch the duck getting up
from the river at dusk,
the catkins' pale fall.

Today at the house,
his jacket and shirt
are stretched on the line,
his dog watches out.
None of us speaks.
Nobody comes.

Comfort

for Joan McBreen

You followed me into the kitchen
where my mother sat in the fall of light from the window,
not looking up.

Ma, I said, *this is Joan.*
This is the woman I spoke of,
the one who steps into the hush of churches

lighting flames against the darkness for you
although she doesn't know you
and it's three months since he died.

She looked up then, her face bright,
her hands lifting and reaching in welcome,
and I woke with the tears on my face.

After My Father Died

The sky didn't fall.

It stayed up there,
luminous, tattered with crows,
all through
January's short days,
February's short days.

Now the year
creeps towards March.
Damp days, grass springing.
The poplars' bare branches
are fruited with starlings and thrushes.
The world is the body of God.
And we —
you, me, him, the starlings and thrushes —
we are all buried here,
mouths made of clay,
mouths filled with clay,
we are all buried here, singing.

Rain in April

I was squatting beside Carmel's lilies of the valley,
poking with my finger, loosening the soil,
providing a bit of encouragement
for the wands of white bells they're about to make,
bells with a scent on them thick as a wall,
a scent that would drown you in remembrance,
when suddenly the April wind rose up and dumped
a pouring of silver-grey rain on my back and my head
and I saw him run for the house but I stayed,
liking the cold wetness and the sudden rip
of the wind rocking the birch and sounding
the wooden chimes in the *malus japonica*,
a tree that is being daily denuded
of its rose-red buds by the bullfinches that we watch
as we sit in bed drinking morning tea and marvelling
at their crunch and spill of tender bud all around,
then speak of the sense in shooting them as my grand-
  mother did,
lining their shameless plumage up in the sights
of her single-barrelled shotgun, dropping them
out of as-yet-unstripped apple trees, the same grandmother
who planted my childhood with lilies of the valley.
So I was squatting there, and everything was thin —
thin grass, thin light, thin buds, thin leafing of trees,
thin cloud moving fast over thin smoke-blue of the
  mountain —
and I knew this thinness for promise-to-be-delivered,
lovelier even than May — the promise delivered —
like the thinness of some people who never quite settle here,
never grow solid and fixed in the world,
                                        and *Yes*, I was thinking,
April is like this, some people are like this, in a minute or two

the rain will pass over, the light will fill out,
and this strange thin moment that's see-through to somewhere
else
will have bowled away off with the rainy wind up the
valley —

Flow

That morning, the drive through rain down the twisted road.
Wild cherry, its scatter of blossom and leaves, its windy
    spaces.
One swallow dipping ahead, the first you've seen,
you following in the scoop of air between bare hedges.

Then, the white room under the eaves, the fire,
the wind sounding an old sound in the chimney.
The jam jar on the mantelpiece, its few leaves,
its criss-cross of unopened bluebells scoring the wall.
Day-candles: the sound-thread as the wax runs off
in quick stream onto the dark hearthstone.
The opened heart, its fragrance in the undefended light
that pours in white draught through the old, thin windows,
while outside, far below, in long wet grass,
the pheasant's coloured strut, his mating call.

All gone, all yesterday, the bluebells all long over,
dead bees lie out on every shelf and table;
glossed seed-pods wither dry, then harden.
Nothing to hold, no ground beneath the feet,
only the days, their passing. One. Another.

Trapped Swallow

The trees are quiet and moist, they stand
attentive as good children in new clothes,
hands folded before them. I have washed
the blanket and am struggling to heave
its damp mass over the yellow plastic of the line.
It was marked with the swallow's panic,
the swallow I found in the stairwell,
exploding off ceilings and doors;
I caught up with it at last,
scrabbling the window behind a row of pot plants,
closed my hand on its air-light life,
opened a door and threw it up into the sky. My life
is small and I would have it
no other way. The first whitethorn
has broken and martins flicker and skim. Last night,
by the river, I noted the scream of the swifts.
Two grey herons rose up from the bank
and went lumbering into the trees.
Further down, the raven flung
its harsh cry from the woods. It broke
and circled, its blunt wings drubbing the air. A little wind
has come up now, out of nowhere, and with it
a misting of rain. I reverse my heave and pull
at the blanket's felt. With the swallow
suddenly quiet in my hand
I felt the weight of privilege: my dense flesh sheltering
its weightless life. This privilege
crept into my sleep and I woke with it
today. I have this small, deep pain
of understanding nothing. The spring is changing
into summer and I keep adding
years to my life.

Wet Summer

The patience of June flowers.
Their wait in the stained silence before rain.

Foxgloves. Their purple towers.
A thousand, thousand miles to Babel.

~

Rain comes. A thousand, thousand drops
upon a thousand, thousand leaves. Their voices.

And all the towers of our Babeled lives
shine quiet and green in gardens.

Rain ceases.
Birds begin.

Sleep in Summer

Light wakes us — there's the sun
climbing the mountains' rim, spilling across the valley,
finding our faces.
It is July,
            between the hay and harvest,
a time at arm's length from all other time,
the roads ragged with meadowsweet and mallow,
with splays of seedheads, slubbed and course: rough linen.
The fields above the house, clotted with sheep all spring,
are empty now and froth with flowering grasses,
still in the morning light. Birds move around
the leafy fields, the leafy garden.

It is the time
to set aside all vigil, good or ill,
to loosen the fixed gaze of our attention
as dandelions let seedlings to the wind.
Wake with the light.
Get up and go about the day,
its surfaces that brighten with the sun;
remark the weight of your hands,
your foot in its sandal,
the lavender's blue hum.

And later, when the light is drowsed and heavy,
go find the burdened fruit trees
and the shade all splashed and opened-out
across the ground.
Spread over it a quilt worn soft by other bodies,
then curl and fall down into sleep in light.

Awaken to a world of long, loose grass-stems,
leaves above,
and birds, breaking out of the leaves.

Sheep Fair Day

'The real aim is not to see God in all things, it is that God, through us, should see the things that we see.'

— Simone Weil

I took God with me to the sheep fair. I said, 'Look,
there's Liv, sitting on the wall, waiting;
these are pens, these are sheep,
this is their shit we are walking in, this is their fear.
See that man over there, stepping along the low walls
between pens, eyes always watching,
mouth always talking, he is the auctioneer.
That is wind in the ash trees above, that is sun
splashing us with running light and dark.
Those men over there, the ones with their faces sealed,
are buying or selling. Beyond in the ring
where the beasts pour in, huddle and rush,
the hoggets are auctioned in lots.
And that woman with the ruddy face and the home-cut hair
and a new child on her arm, that is how it is to be woman
with the milk running, sitting on wooden boards
in this shit-milky place of animals and birth and death
as the bidding rises and falls.'

Then I went back outside and found Fintan.
I showed God his hand as he sat on the rails,
how he let it trail down and his fingers played
in the curly back of a ewe. Fintan's a sheep-man,
he's deep into sheep, though it's cattle he keeps now,
for sound commercial reasons.
'Feel that,' I said,
'feel with my heart the force in that hand
that's twining her wool as he talks.'
Then I went with Fintan and Liv to Refreshments,
I let God sip tea, boiling hot, from a cup,

and I lent God my fingers to feel how they burned
when I tripped on a stone and it slopped.
'This is hurt,' I said, 'there'll be more.'
And the morning wore on and the sun climbed
and God felt how it is when I stand too long,
how the sickness rises, how the muscles burn.

Later, at the back end of the afternoon,
I went down to swim in the green slide of river,
I worked my way under the bridge, against the current,
then I showed how it is to turn onto your back
with, above you and a long way up, two gossiping pigeons,
and a clump of valerian, holding itself to the sky.
I remarked on the stone arch as I drifted through it,
how it dapples with sunlight from the water,
how the bridge hunkers down, crouching low in its tracks
and roars when a lorry drives over.

And later again, in the kitchen,
wrung out, at day's ending, and empty,
I showed how it feels
to undo yourself,
to dissolve, and grow age-old, nameless:

woman sweeping a floor, darkness growing.

Flying Across Land Mass

Those loose blue blooms
that drift
under fluffs of white cloud —

On Derry's Walls

'A thing can be explained only by that which is more subtle than itself; there is nothing subtler than love: by what then can love be explained?'

— Sumnûn ibn Hamza al-Muhibb

The blackbird that lives in the graveyard
sits on the Wall at the fade of the winter day.
He has fed off the worms that have fed off the clay
of the Protestant dead.

And yet he is subtle,
subtle and bright
as the love that might explain him
yet may not be explained.

As for the rest, there is almost nothing to add,
not even *This is how it was,*
because all we can ever say
is *This is how it looked to me* —

In the blackbird's looped entrails
everything is resolved.

Sunflowers

for Valentina Gherman-Tazlauanu

LE CHEVAL

The thing I like most about Switzerland —
great unfenced fields of sunflowers
dying in the light.

When we run out of broken-language conversation
we play 'What animal would you be?'
'Un cheval,' she says, quick and soft.

The things I like most about horses —
their strong necks, the planes of their faces,
the way the life sits inside them.

The things I like most about Valentina —
her feminine hands, weight-bearing shoulders,
the way her face lights.

Those sunflowers. It's not because they are dying —
dying things fill me with grief —
but I like their bowed heads and that moulded place

where the neck flows into the nape.
Standing so straight, whole armies at prayer
before the last battle is lost.

I DON'T GO TO THE SUNFLOWER FIELD

The rain is falling on the trees and on the vines,
falling on draggled sunflower fields.
It beats on the long windows
that hold such blank and tender rectangles
when they stand open in late August dusk.

ONE SUNFLOWER

I am in the sunflower field.
I reach up my hands for a sunflower —
this loveliest of all gestures,
more tender with no kiss.

It is dumb and beautiful,
moon-faced, staring, shy;
larger than any other face
I've ever drawn to mine.

AWAY FROM HOME

The sky is piled high over the sunflower field,
onion-domed,
sweaty with drifting vapours, blue and grey.
Peculiar landscape. First the sunflowers,
then dark trees, then Lake Geneva,
then mountains in a blue line, the French Alps.
Then all this sky.
Up and up and up.
Yesterday I learned the Polish way of saying Conrad:
YOU-SEPH KOR-SHEN-YOVSKI.
I had to say it over and over, slowly,
making shapes my mouth doesn't want to make.
Afterwards, I went upstairs to find myself.
I tried to work, gave up, put things away.
I washed a shirt, then rinsed out my black knickers.
I draped them over the golden neck
of a bath tap shaped like a swan.

Each night I wish the others *Bonne nuit* early.
I sit in the dark with the gilded swan and the window
watching the inside of the onion dome
threaded with the moving lights of planes.
For the life of me
I can't understand human beings. How we must always
be going somewhere busily, or coming back,
filling the air with sounds, saying the same word differently,
making bath taps mock at what they're not.
And I don't understand why it makes me so bewildered,
this piling of one thing hard upon another,
this planting of sunflowers, straight-lined in square fields.

ENOUGH

I want to stay in one place for a long time.
I don't care if there aren't any sunflowers.
I want to see the same thing every morning.
I want to rest in the same people.

AFTERNOON RAIN

The sound of the rain
falling straight and thick

in the green light. The soft
susurration of the fan

like breath.
I lie on the bed

loosening the pins
of the mind's grip.

The pins fall out,
the walls dissolve,

I tread the hem
of Valentina's dream.

My feet are slippered
in ochre-coloured felt.

Ottoman slippers.
They do not tear or stain.

ELEVENTH OF SEPTEMBER

We passed the sunflower field without a glance.
We strolled through straight-lined vineyards
robbing grapes.

Valentina was pro-active.
She said she'd never do this in Moldova.
Mais en Suisse —
She shrugged and laughed a joyous laugh.

We slid our hands behind us when we heard their voices.
When we saw them, they too hid their hands.
She laughed again. *Ils sont les voleurs, comme nous.*

Back at the Chateau, she went off to change for the
  Reception.
Darius told me. I ran upstairs, knocked on her door.
She wore a satin dressing-gown. She listened
and her face was white.

Le Château de Lavigny,
Switzerland

She Hasn't Been Paid for Six Months

I'm with Valentina in the kitchen.
She tells me there's a problem with her e-mail.
The office of the journal that she edits
is in the National Library of Moldova
which hasn't paid the phone bill.
It's only temporary, it will soon be sorted.

Of course we know these things about these countries.
But somehow it is different in the kitchen
when she is slicing up tomatoes
and you are ironing your blue blouse.
You see her forehead knit, then clear.
She is assuring you the problem won't last long.

Saint Fursey's Song

St Fursey speaks to his brothers, St Ultan and St Foillan

Come, brothers,
we are free now, let us live freely,
the rose and the fire in our hearts.

Let us not worry our heads over rightness or wrongness,
nor fret about goodness,
but sing like the birds in the trees.

And we will go wandering, following the light,
we will speak where we will, and sleep where we will,
and take no more care than the lilies in His book.

I made enquiries of that olive-skinned young man,
he who studies under Cumian
and comes from a place he calls Lebanon;

he tells me these lilies spring up like our orchids —
fair and careless and singing with colour —
and we three will be like them and will walk

with easy steps even in the darkest, most fearsome of places,
and certainly we will fear,
but underneath our fear we will be fearless.

So let us take up our ash-plants and be off,
and you, Ultan, bring that pup if you cannot leave her,
she will lift up your heart when your feet are sore,

she may even bring us a bird for the pot but I doubt it,
I think she is not of the stuff of great hunters.
And you, Foillan, tell your crow to follow after,

and sometimes to go before us to show us the way,
for he is a ruffianly bird, full of appetite and hard sense,
and it's well that men like us be watched for by such as him.

Now farewell, Ireland, loveliest of all earth's lands.
We may never more see you with human eyes,
but know that we will always have sight of you in our
hearts.

And farewell to all who dwell in this land,
do not fear for us, for our souls are safe,
and what are our bodies but little sod houses

putting shelter round fire and round love?
What harm then if the house should crumble?
Fire and love cannot crumble,

fire and love will burn always
in one house or another
lighting windows in the darkest night.

Saints Fursey, Ultan and Foillan, three brothers who were born in Ireland, went to England sometime around 630, and founded a monastery at Burgh Castle near Yarmouth. When the monastery was destroyed by the Mercians, Ultan and Foillan followed Fursey who had gone to Gaul sometime earlier, founding monasteries at Lagny, Fosse and Peronne. Foillan had great success converting the Brabantes. He was murdered by forest outlaws in 655. Fursey and Ultan died in 648 and 686 respectively.

In Age

When they say my name
I go to them, my hand outstretched.
It is taken, I am led,
more led than in childhood.

My father draws me to him, shows me things.
My mother calls me and I walk with her.
My given name takes on a greenness
it has never held for me before.

Achill

ACHILL SEPTEMBER

for Richard Dore

On this island of bones and stones
I catch myself planning
the leaving of gardens.

This urge
to live hunkered into the wind.

On the strand
a new-dead porpoise, then a headless turtle.
A leatherback.
Its big, hinged backbone
working loose from its meat.

The hills
pull free from their moorings,
they drift off under
the vast sky.

Suddenly I'm remembering
the float of sweet peas in Kilkenny dusk.

Apples,
each fruit twisting into the hand.
And wasps,
gorging.

Bones
are gathered here like flowers.

They cut black sods and stack them tight
against the roar of winter.

FLIGHT

That day it was black all day.
Black sky, black bog, black heave of the sea,
black trees rattling in the black wind.

All the farm men and women that have ever broken ground
  in me
raised a great shout that I should leave this place,
leave this black land.

THE HILL BEHIND THE HOUSE

Each morning here I go to the back window
to check the colour of the sky above the hill.

It is a good hill, small and close and brown,
its loose curve hardly breaking water.

When there is blue behind this arc
it goes on up forever.

When there is thick-and-grey
I know a finite world of bog and sheep,

plain and familiar, a damp sedgy place
that stills the heart till it rests clean and bare.

ON KEEL STRAND

There was a big old woman
and I stared at her and stared
because I wanted to learn how to live in age
without being pinched;
she had strong white legs and bare feet and windy white hair
and behind her the swimmers dipped and plunged,
and behind them the black-rubber surfers
stood to the flashing sea;
and all her clothes were loose
with a blown cotton blue-and-whiteness,
and in her hand was a red bucket;
and all around her,
and in the spaces and gaps of arms and legs and fingers,
was a wash of green sea — not bulky, not flesh, not fixed,
but moving and pouring
and growing more translucent and transparent
as she grew denser —
and under her big, white, splay-toed feet
the sand was fine and greyish
and damp where the tide had slid off,
and I looked down at my bare legs
with the first blue vein wriggling the calf
and my feet planted in the wash like saplings
and the mystery of flesh was very near and very far,
it was all and yet nothing at all.

THE CALLIGRAPHY OF BIRDS

Sands scribbled with the scurryings of waders,
scored by strut-marks of the blackbacks,
printed with the stalk of a grey heron.

Little flocks, flickering the tideline,
the cold glide of the blackbacks,
the heron's loose-winged float against the sea.

LIKE SEA GLASS

for Will

After his son was married we went to the island.
The journey was long and we brought with us all of the
  pictures.
We carried them over the causeway and skirted the mountains,
passed the bog and the black shine of water, then came to the
  ocean.

There we knelt among stones and unpacked them, one at a time,
the cherishing muslin parting and falling apart in our hands.
When the wooden boxes were emptied, the rabble of
  packaging
flew on the wind and we cast the crates into the sea.

Then we lifted the images high and processed them before
  us —
faded prints, oils crackled and scorched in the heat of the fire,
icons that shone in the wavering light of the candles,
garlanded photographs, swagged with white tulle.

The waves were a wall on the sky; they curled in green glass.
Spume clouded the surfaces, misted the varnish,
the wind and the crying of curlews whipped away words,
salt cut the perfume of incense and flowers.

At first we had eyes and hands for our task alone
but the winter light shone on the pearly sheen of the water
so we set down the pictures and faced to the sea,
and when we turned back they were dimmed and ground
  down.

GATHERING STONES

That woman, walking, day after day,
on the afternoon shore, heaving up finds
from a bank of grey stones,
by the rattle and drag
of the sea.

Stones — one at a time —
discarding the treasure she holds,
nesting the next
in that place
between belly and breast —

And I want to tell her
to leave off this handling of bones,
to search out the tiny blue bells
on the milkwort stems in the dunes
(our business being flesh)

but find myself so empty
from all this stone washed in sea-light
that there is almost nothing left to say
and my few words come
separate and stranded,

as pebbles set down by the tide.

Remember This

All week it's been warm
and the thistledown blows in the wind.
It bowls up the roads,
it drifts the ripe fields,
it wanders about in the hall.

The raven sits high in the Scots pine
in the wane of the afternoon.
Chock, chock, he says in his slate-grey voice,
chock, chock, the end of summer.
Who cares, I say. *Full up*, I say,

the earth breathes plenty,
the thistles release on the wind.

Glory

Sycamore,
running with gold leaves
in a small wind
from a damp sky.

And behind it,
dark haws
on a thorn,
its leaves cast.

So comes glory,
and who cares,
so we
shine like this

even for one hour,
even for one eye,
opening only
one heart?

September Dusk

The high and ragged yellow daisies
crowd and lean and blow.
The darkening leaves rush together.

I lift the spent day in my fingers,
as a woman lifts skirts over water.

Night comes.
My hand opens slackly,
lets fall the folds of cloth.

October

The butterflies are stretched
on the walls and on the sills,
they have spread their wings out quietly to die.

The poplars make their water-sound,
the wooden chimes their *chock-chock* sound;
the turning leaves gleam in the stormy light.

Changing, all things changing,
going down into the darkness,
and the river running shining to the sea.

Tent

for Seán

He set up the tent before he went trekking in Georgia,
slept there a couple of times, practising,

then off he went. It was August. I was here alone.
The first three nights I looked out from the window

at the small red dome in the orchard under the trees,
then I went to bed in our bed.

The fourth saw me in pyjamas
carrying a sleeping bag out, crawling in.

Then I lay on my belly, looking about me —
the apple trees, heavy with dusk and unripe fruit,

and the house, away off at the top of the garden,
black against the half-dark summer sky.

In the night the rain came, loud on the flysheet,
I woke and slept and woke and slept again.

Come morning I rolled over, opened the zip,
threw back the flaps.

The house was where it had been.
Unchanged. Sufficient to itself.

I felt released from it and easy
down there with the bright, damp trees.

For two more nights I slept there, telling no one,
then went back inside to our bed.

~

Now it's November.
I dig leeks for the table in the gloom.

I like being out. The wind and the mud,
and the lit house shining through the dusk.

I like its yellow warmth, and how I'm off from it,
no longer snugly dressed in my own life.

Perhaps, as for him, it's a sort of rehearsal. Perhaps
I'm practising for when I am unfleshed and free.

Winter Heart

Winter again, and I'm glad that the seasons
keep coming around and around.
I am glad that the heart, too, is seasonal,
that it loses its leaves in November,
holds trembling hands to the sky;
that it freezes and thaws and freezes,
running with water in autumn,
singing with birds in the spring.

It is ready again now for darkness
and a night-sky splintered with stars,
for winds, wuthering its stony ramparts,
for fire in the halls within.

When Maura had Died

for Carmel

These days —
                                   filled with wonder of death.

This morning I woke early,
watched the day come, blue and hard-won,
the rain's clean shine on the glass, the drops
on the crossbar hanging in the light.
I knew dailiness, saw birds
moving across the window, saw the window
for a portal, as in Renaissance painting.

I never knew
that death was this simple;
you left
as a woman holding a letter
moves to the light —

Then I wanted the grace
to share the open secret,
to be wasp in the apple and apple arching
around the devouring wasp,
sheltering its feeding. Oh, let me live living,
devoured and devouring,
eating myself down
to my own core.

Where to Call Home

i.m. Maura McNally

This living is sometimes
like following a death,
as sorrowful and the same
sweetness, heart gone
to some other place.

I have been reading
Tess Gallagher, the high pride
of her mourning, her knowing there is nothing
for her here, yet here she will stay,
living, even sharply alive
to life, its frail beauty,
frailer and lovelier still since Carver's death.

Some men need deserts,
some women tend children like candles,
our dog lays her face on Seán's thigh,
her deepest place.
Myself, I blow in the wind,
living nowhere except in the world, which is all holy,
loving windows and doorways. Daylight,
its fall through clear glass.

Daniel's Duck

for Frances

I held out the shot mallard, she took it from me,
looped its neck-string over a drawer of the dresser.
The children were looking on, half-caught.
Then the kitchen life — warm, lit, glowing —
moved forward, taking in the dead bird,
and its coldness, its wildness, were leaching away.

The children were sitting to their dinners.
Us too — drinking tea, hardly noticing
the child's quiet slide from his chair,
his small absorbed body before the duck's body,
the duck changing — feral, live —
arrowing up out of black sloblands
with the gleam of a river
falling away below.

Then the duck — dead again — hanging from the drawer-
knob,
the green head, brown neck running into the breast,
the intricate silvery-greyness of the back;
the wings, their white bars and blue flashes,
the feet, their snakey, orange scaliness, small claws, piteous
webbing,
the yellow beak, blooded,
the whole like a weighted sack —
all that downward-dragginess of death.

He hovered, took a step forward, a step back,
something appeared in his face, some knowledge
of a place where he stood, the world stilled,
the lit streaks of sunrise running off red
into the high bowl of morning.

She watched him, moving to touch, his hand out:
What is it, Daniel, do you like the duck?
He turned as though caught in the act,
saw the gentleness in her face and his body loosened.
I thought there was water on it —
he was finding the words, one by one,
holding them out, to see would they do us —
but there isn't.
He added this on, going small with relief
that his wing-drag of sounds was enough.

Dublin Train, Solstice

for my father

There's a cold sky and gulls in the new ploughing
and ice on the stretched water glazing the fields.
The year's nearly done, and I've not once taken this train till
now,
not sat at this window, back facing the future,
watching the landscape unravel into what's gone.
Your death knocked the thrive out of me,
knocked the thrive out of the year as well.
The sky is spreading itself out and breaking open
and I'm tired of fretting the mind over mysteries,
am nearly ready to give up and not understand.
This wraith-mooned daylight is thin and cold
as the smell of a lemon.
There's an ash by a wall in a field above our house.
I go there in winter to find you in the empty branches,
in the way the tree stands to the sky. The dogs quarter,
snouts dropped to the smell that has them by the nose.
I'm not far off that myself — hard on the scent
when the bird has gone. This is the fiercest week of the year,
this descent into dark, into the formless heart of matter.
Our souls enter our bodies, hungry for experience,
they run us around like the mice that live in the skirting
and skitter across the floorboards in the stillness,
their quick, sure darts scoring the emptiness behind the eyes.

Day's Ending

We quiet ourselves, expecting the night.
We have left ourselves, await ourselves,
in this place between. Life moves
in the room, becomes more itself
each moment we let it alone.

This, our best chance
at absence while present,
the time we least feel
our weight pressing in on us.

We long for this,
yet cannot bear it for long.
One of us always
rises, walks over, turns on the lights.

Acknowledgements

Acknowledgements are due to the editors of the following publications in which some of these poems, or versions of them, have appeared: *The Black Mountain Review*, *HU*, *The Missouri Review*, *The Recorder*, *ROPES*, *The Stinging Fly*, *The Sunday Tribune*, *Tabla*, *TriQuarterly* and *The Women's Studies Review*, NUI Galway.

The author records grateful thanks to An Chomhairle Ealaíon/The Arts Council, Ireland, Le Château de Lavigny, Switzerland, the Heinrich Böll Cottage, Achill, and the Tyrone Guthrie Centre at Annaghmakerrig.